The Messiah Revealed in Prophecy

By Cushroo Bejon

WIPF & STOCK · Eugene, Oregon

Wipf and Stock Publishers
199 W 8th Ave, Suite 3
Eugene, OR 97401

The Messiah Revealed in Prophecy
By Bejon, Cushroo
Copyright©2019 Apostolos
ISBN 13: 978-1-5326-8094-6
Publication date 2/1/2019
Previously published by Apostolos, 2019

This is the plan determined for the whole world; this is the hand stretched out over all nations. For the Lord Almighty has purposed, and who can thwart him? His hand is stretched out, and who can turn it back? (Isa 14:26–27)

Author's Preface

Following the publication of my first book, The Word of God in our Hands (see Bibliography), I have been motivated to turn my attention to the subject of prophecy in the life of the Messiah. In undertaking this task, I am aware that I am neither an expert in medicine, history, archaeology, linguistics or mathematics, all of which are embraced by my subject. I often find that commentators and scholars prefer to place their speculations and interpretations above the plain truth of the Word of God.

You will find some references to this practice further on in this book whereas, as indicated in my previous book, I am firmly convinced that the Word of God as we have it today is an accurate and reliable copy of God's words revealed to men. But I am greatly encouraged by the words that Jesus uttered, even after many had rejected Him, "I thank you, Father, Lord of heaven and earth, because you have hidden these things from the wise and learned, and revealed them to little children." (Matt 11:25).

This truth is reinforced by recalling that when Jesus started His work on Earth, He chose fishermen, not the learned rabbis He had met in the temple at Jerusalem, and He taught them "the secret of the kingdom of God" (Mark 4:11). So I look to Him, my Heavenly Father, to teach me what I need to know about Him (John 14:26) and to enable me to distinguish between what is from God and what is from man. Since the world in its fallen wisdom has rejected God (1 Cor 1:22), God has declared, "I will destroy the wisdom of the wise; the intelligence of the intelligent I will frustrate" (1 Cor 1:19). The world even denies God the title of Creator, let alone recognising Him as Redeemer and Lord, whereas we are not of the world any more than our Lord is (John 15:19).

I need to indicate clearly that I am not disparaging the value of education, having been involved in it for many years and recognising that it is necessary to understand differing viewpoints. However, an educational qualification is not in itself an entitlement to teach in biblical matters. It follows, therefore, that it is a mistake to think that biblical exposition which is done by people having academic qualifications is of necessity biblically correct.

Complicated expositions, relying on man's wisdom and involving speculation to make explanations more plausible and in line with current thinking can never be preferable to the plain truth of God's Word, however unpalatable the result may appear. By God's grace and goodness to me, I have been a Christian reading God's Word for more than 70 years, and I have found the Word of God to be entirely trustworthy. The Scripture itself encourages us to test everything, and "hold on to what is good" (1 Thess 5:21). In the words of Sir Frederick Kenyon, the time has come "to shake off the excessive criticism characteristic of much biblical scholarship in the latter half of the 19th century, and to restore confidence in the Bible as a guide to truth and a basis for the conduct of life" (from The Bible and Modern Scholarship).

Once again, I am grateful to my wife Jane, for typing and presentation support, my son James for discussions and my church minister, Andrew Grey, Immanuel Church Brentwood, under whose ministry the Word of God has been honoured and obeyed. I alone am responsible for what is written.

THE MESSIAH REVEALED IN PROPHECY

In addition to predicting the future, prophecy reveals God in the Scriptures, in at least three further areas:

1. Predictive revelation of God's truth with warnings of impending judgment for those who remain unrepentant. This can be seen in the account of Jonah and the city of Nineveh, which on excavation in 1845 revealed evidences of the vast city described in the Book of Jonah. The king of Israel was similarly told by the prophet Jeremiah to surrender the besieged city of Jerusalem to Nebuchadnezzar, king of Babylon, and accept their deportation to Babylon in 597 BCE as punishment by God for their sins.

2. Prophetic revelations that brought to light hidden secrets. The planned deceit of Ananias and Sapphira was exposed in Acts chapter 5 and similarly the greed in the heart of Simon the Sorcerer was unmasked in Acts chapter 8. On the other hand, Paul was able to assure the shipwrecked sailors that an angel of God had shown him that in spite of the shipwreck, all their lives would be safeguarded (Acts chapter 27). Simeon and Anna had also been shown by the Holy Spirit that before they departed this life they would see the Lord's anointed Messiah even though He was only a baby and this was fulfilled as He had said. Simeon's memorable words stand out here, "Sovereign Lord, as you have promised, you may now dismiss your servant in peace. For my eyes have seen your salvation" (Luke 2:29–30).

3. To impart an understanding of God's actions and thereby prepare the hearers for what God was doing. Peter was to be sifted as wheat by Satan, but Jesus had prayed for his restoration so that when he had recovered, he could strengthen his brothers (Luke 22:32). Jesus warned His disciples of increasing persecution so that they might know and accept that this was God's plan and purpose and they would not subsequently fall away (John 16:1, 4). The unbelief of the Jews was foreordained by God and prophesied by Isaiah when he saw the glory of Jesus and spoke about Him, and so the Jews rejected Jesus as their Messiah (John 12:39–41).

We always have the assurance that what God has said through His prophets will come to pass. Sometimes we will see certain events and situations threatening to prevent what God has said will happen from happening, but we will always find that God's purposes will be fulfilled by one means or another. Even denial, betrayal and death by crucifixion were made to fulfil the Divine purposes ordained from eternity. The closing section of this book traces the prophecies concerning the resurrection and exaltation of the Messiah to the throne of honour at the right hand of the Majesty on High. Finally, we will see Him in that momentous event that will rock the world, as He takes His place to rule the world in glory and power as King of Kings and Lord of Lords.

God's Plan Unfolding

Amongst the things that we need to be reminded of, Peter emphasises, are the power and the coming of our Lord Jesus Christ (2 Pet 1:12–21). The majesty and glory of the Lord Jesus Christ is the authority with which Peter is addressing them. Uppermost in this section is the vision of the glory and majesty of Jesus as He receives the Divine accolade, "This is my Son, whom I love; with him I am well pleased" (verse 17). Of this event, the writer emphasises he was an eye-witness when Jesus was revealed in His majestic glory at the transfiguration. Also at the transfiguration were James and John, fellow eye-witnesses of Jesus in His glory, just as I believe that those who are His will see Him when we are with Him in glory.

Two factors are indicated here to authenticate the truth of Christian prophecy. The <u>first</u> is that prophecy is not a story cleverly invented by man to deceive, but rather it comes from the mouth of prophets (verse 19) who are sent by God. Thus, Peter aptly describes prophecy as, "a light shining in a dark place, until the day dawns and the morning star rises in your hearts" (verse 19). When the rule of God is once again established on the earth, the darkness will be banished (like the freezing and death of Narnia was banished by Aslan), as the light of Jesus will shine in darkened hearts.

The <u>second</u> fact stated is that though prophecy came through the prophets, they were not the ones who interpreted it (verse 20). In fact, even though they searched intently and with the greatest care, the time and circumstances of the fulfilment of their prophecies were not made known to them. Instead they were shown by the Holy Spirit that the Messiah would suffer and be humiliated but ultimately, He would be glorified. It was also revealed to them that these revelations were not given for their benefit but for those of us who would believe the gospel in subsequent generations (verses 11 to 12). The prophet, therefore, was the mouthpiece of God. He was guided and controlled by the power of the Holy Spirit to utter or pen the thoughts that God had given him and the Holy Spirit safeguarded him so that he uttered or penned only God's truth. I am not convinced of the view sometimes expressed that individual writers of the Scripture writings were themselves theologians who shaped their writings in keeping with the group or church to which they belonged. When inspired by the Holy Spirit such men were guided and directed what to write, they were not acting independently of the Holy Spirit.

Prediction and Fulfilment

Matthew has been particularly led by the Holy Spirit to emphasise the connection between prophecy and fulfilment. All the Gospel writers, but especially Matthew, emphasise this relationship in the life and death of Jesus the Messiah. In the birth narrative of the Messiah there is a closely interconnected series of events which not only must occur in a certain order but each event itself is dependent on several other independent events. Despite man's evil and the devil's attempts to break this sequence and even destroy the Messiah Himself, we see the overseeing Father protect His child, His beloved Son, from any possible harm. When we are dealing with secular predictions there could be a significant lack of correlation between prediction and fulfilment. But when we are dealing with biblical prediction and fulfilment the correlation is complete because the Word of the Lord ensures that this occurs. The plan made from eternity began to come into operation at the fall of man in the Garden of Eden. The key phrase that would initiate the plan of God's salvation was:

> He will crush your head, and you will strike his heel (Gen 3:15c).

God had already planned to crush this virulent enemy and though more than 4000 years elapsed, the death of the Messiah on the cross of Calvary was the first fatal blow in the crushing defeat of the devil. This will be followed more than 3000 years later after the 1000-year millennium when that dragon, the ancient serpent, who is the devil will be finally thrown together with the beast and false prophet into the lake of burning sulphur. There they will be tormented day and night for ever and ever (Rev 20:10). The Messiah entered our world as a helpless babe in the care of His Almighty Father. Every step of the plan was carefully made and all this took place to fulfil what the Lord had said through the prophet Isaiah:

> Behold, the virgin will conceive and give birth to a son, and will call him Immanuel. (Isa 7:14)

At this point we need to consider the prophecies concerning three giants and pioneers of the faith,

Abraham, Moses and Jacob. Abraham's previous name was Abram ("exalted father") but God changed his name to Abraham ("father of many") in view of the purpose God had planned for Abraham. He was instructed to leave his home town, Ur of the Chaldees, and in obedience to God's command he went to a land that God would show him. He became aware that he was on a mission under God's directions, building altars in the places where God appeared to him, as he journeyed through the land of Canaan calling on God in worship and prayer. He came under the influence of powerful and unscrupulous rulers and made many mistakes, but God's hand protected and blessed him as he journeyed from place to place.

Not only was Abraham a pivotal character in God's purposes to bring the Messiah into our world but because the changes that God was asking Abraham to make were so life-changing, God frequently repeated His promises to Abraham. God's promise to Abraham was:

> I will make you into a great nation, and I will bless you; I will make your name great, and you will be a blessing. I will bless those who bless you, and whoever curses you I will curse; and all peoples on earth will be blessed through you. (Gen 12:2–3)

In His grace and as part of His Divine purpose, God added that all-important final clause, "and all peoples on earth will be blessed through you." So, about 2000 years before it was due to happen, we have Abraham being given the promise that One born in his family would be the means of blessing to all the people on the earth. Abraham probably did not understand how all nations on the earth would be blessed through him, but he believed and therefore:

> Without weakening in his faith, he faced the fact that his body was as good as dead—since he was about a hundred years old—and that Sarah's womb was also dead. Yet he did not waver through unbelief regarding the promise of God, but was strengthened in his faith and gave glory to God. (Rom 4:19–20)

This promise to Abraham was fulfilled in the coming of Christ so that both Jew and Gentile as members of one body, the church of Christ, may come into God's presence with freedom, confidence and unity.

As God was bringing Israel into the promised land, He wanted them to be different from the nations around them, since those nations freely practised idolatry, sorcery and divination. Moses was also given the promise as part of God's purpose:

> I will raise up for them a prophet like you from among their fellow Israelites, and I will put my words in his mouth. He will tell them everything I command him. I myself will call to account anyone who does not listen to my words that the prophet speaks in my name. (Deut 18:18–19)

Jesus is like the prophet Moses, because He shares in our humanity, having flesh and blood like us (Hebrews 2:14). Also He fulfils perfectly the prediction that He would communicate God to us, because we read these definitive words of Jesus, "These words you hear are not my own; they belong to the Father who sent me" (John 14:24).

Jacob was next in the prophetic line after Abraham and Isaac but Isaac does not appear to have been very proactive in the Messianic succession. He not only sought but also inherited the birthright that his older brother, Esau, despised and sold to him for a plate of pottage. The first of the prophecies given to Jacob was:

> There above it stood the Lord, and he said: "I am the Lord, the God of your father Abraham and the God of Isaac. I will give you and your descendants the land on which you are lying. Your descendants will be like the dust of the earth, and you will spread out to the west and to the east, to the north and to the south. All peoples on earth will be blessed through you and your offspring. (Gen 28:13–14)

Jacob may have now felt that the spiritual dimension was returning to his life after a prolonged period of scheming and acquiring things for himself instead of trusting the God who had chosen him (Gen 28:3–4). Most significantly, the promise made to his grandfather was now being renewed to him, that all the people on the earth would be blessed through his offspring, that is, through the redemptive work achieved in Christ.

Later in his life the time had come for him to pass on the inheritance to the firstborn. Reuben, Jacob's firstborn, had forfeited his right to this (Ge. 49:4) and instead Jacob was moved to nominate Judah as the inheritor of the firstborn's rights, in the words,

> Judah, your brothers will praise you … The scepter will not depart from Judah, nor the ruler's staff from between his feet, until he to whom it belongs shall come and the obedience of the nations shall be his. (Gen 49:8–10)

> "I have installed my king on Zion, my holy mountain." ...
> You will break them with a rod of iron; you will dash them
> to pieces like pottery." Therefore, you kings, be wise; be
> warned, you rulers of the earth. Serve the Lord with fear
> and celebrate his rule with trembling. Kiss his son, or he
> will be angry and your way will lead to your destruction,
> for his wrath can flare up in a moment. Blessed are all who
> take refuge in him. (Ps 2:6, 9–12).

The many aspects of these prophecies are being fulfilled in Christ. The sceptre, the symbol of His authority, and His royal staff, point to the fact that He will rule the nations in righteousness and justice. To Him every knee will bow down and so all, particularly those who oppose Him, are advised not to incur the Son's anger and be destroyed. The day is coming nearer when one like a Son of Man will be given authority, glory and sovereign power over all the nations (Dan 7:13–14).

A further prophecy, though given by Balaam, a soothsayer, describes the ruler who will come out of Jacob:

> I see him, but not now; I behold him, but not near. A star
> will come out of Jacob; a scepter will rise out of Israel. He
> will crush the foreheads of Moab, the skulls of all the
> people of Sheth. (Num 24:17)

Even though Balaam, under the influence of Balak, seems the most unlikely person to convey such a prophecy, he was strictly under God's control (Num 22:13, 18, 20). The star and the sceptre clearly refer to Israel's future Messianic Ruler as He achieves victory over His enemies. It is worth noting that even though Balaam was not the fittest of persons to deliver a prophecy but because he was under the control of the Holy Spirit, the integrity of the prophecy was not compromised. A question that cannot be definitively answered is whether this star that "shall rise out of Israel" is the star which the Magi saw, or is it a reference to Jesus, the "bright Morning Star" (Rev 22:16)?

The Birth of John the Baptist

Key to the coming of the Messiah into our world was the forerunner, John the Baptist, who was sent by God to prepare the way for the coming Messiah. His ministry was prophesied by God more than 700 years before he was born, when God had revealed to the prophet Isaiah the coming of John the Baptist,

> A voice of one calling: "In the wilderness prepare the way for the Lord; make straight in the desert a highway for our God. Every valley shall be raised up, every mountain and hill made low; the rough ground shall become level, the rugged places a plain. And the glory of the Lord will be revealed, and all people will see it together. For the mouth of the Lord has spoken." (Isa 40:3–5)

John's Gospel identifies John the Baptist as the one fulfilling this description, sent from God as a witness to Christ, the Light of the World (John 1:6–9). But when a plan is made there is always the possibility of something unforeseen happening or of something going wrong. Only an all-knowing and almighty person can guarantee the occurrence of an event thousands of years before it is due to occur. At roughly the same time the Messiah who is both God and man was to be born into our world. First, the forerunner John the Baptist was prophetically and miraculously born to a barren couple, Zechariah the priest and his wife Elizabeth. The angel Gabriel announced this to an astounded and unbelieving Zechariah as an answer to their prayers, telling them of the ministry God had chosen for the forerunner even before he was born.

Within six months the same angel Gabriel was sent by God to a virgin named Mary, who was pledged to be married to a man named Joseph. Once again this was shattering news to Mary, drawing out the amazed response, "How will this be, since I am a virgin?" (Luke 1:34). Both Elizabeth and Mary were prophetically informed of these events and both mothers-to-be were deeply aware of the sacred mission for which the Holy Spirit had chosen them, and both of them burst into spontaneous praise to God (Luke 1:42–45, 46–55).

Jesus taught His disciples about the importance of John the Baptist's ministry, declaring him to be His messenger, with the words:

> I will send my messenger, who will prepare the way before me. (Mal 3:1)

Jesus declared John the Baptist to be the greatest prophet, who also fulfilled another prophecy of Malachi:

> See, I will send the prophet Elijah to you before that great and dreadful day of the Lord comes. He will turn the hearts of the parents to their children, and the hearts of the children to their parents; or else I will come and strike the land with total destruction. (Mal 4:5–6)

Also:

> But who can endure the day of his coming? Who can stand when he appears? For he will be like a refiner's fire or a launderer's soap. He will sit as a refiner and purifier of silver; he will purify the Levites and refine them like gold and silver. Then the Lord will have men who will bring offerings in righteousness, and the offerings of Judah and Jerusalem will be acceptable to the Lord, as in days gone by, as in former years. (Mal 3:2–4)

The ministry of John was therefore as a messenger calling upon all Israel, in the words of the prophecy:

> A voice of one calling in the wilderness: "Prepare the way for the Lord; make straight in the desert a highway for our God." (Isa 40:3 margin)

As a result, people from Jerusalem and Judea flocked to him and confessing their sins they were baptised by John in the river Jordan. Even dishonest tax collectors and soldiers came to him to enquire what they should do in keeping with their baptisms. John's ministry was to prepare the people for the coming of Jesus. Many hearts needed to be turned but the work of purification and restoration would be carried out by the Messiah. This was a message of warning and judgement and in keeping with the prophecy John reflected the displeasure of the Lord caused by the sins of the people by calling upon the people to produce fruit in keeping with repentance. John's preparatory work was to be completed by the Messiah chosen by God. These signs were therefore recognised as being those related to the coming Messiah and so John the Baptist, being imprisoned, sought assurance whether Jesus was the coming Messiah. Jesus's reply for John was:

> Jesus replied, "Go back and report to John what you hear and see: The blind receive sight, the lame walk, those who have leprosy are cleansed, the deaf hear, the dead are raised, and the good news is proclaimed to the poor. Blessed is anyone who does not stumble on account of me." (Matt 11:4–6)

This is all in accordance with Isaiah's prophecies (Isa 35:5–6; 61:1–3).

The Lineage of David

In connection with the birth of the Messiah there is frequent reference to the fact that the Messiah would be of the lineage of David. The origin of the connection between the house of David and the Messiah, who would redeem Israel, can be seen in these prophecies:

> Now you have been pleased to bless the house of your servant, that it may continue forever in your sight; for you, Lord, have blessed it, and it will be blessed forever. (1 Chron 17:27)

> His line will continue forever and his throne endure before me like the sun; it will be established forever like the moon, the faithful witness in the sky. (Ps 89:36–37)

> A shoot will come up from the stump of Jesse; from his roots a Branch will bear fruit. The Spirit of the Lord will rest on him—the Spirit of wisdom and of understanding, the Spirit of counsel and of might, the Spirit of the knowledge and fear of the Lord. (Isa 11:1–2)

Both Matthew's and Luke's Gospels trace the genealogy of Jesus to David for this reason and we are often reminded that Jesus is of "the Root of David" (Rev 5:5; 22:16). God has fulfilled His promise to David. Amongst the very memorable prophecies is:

> For to us a child is born, to us a son is given, and the government will be on his shoulders. And he will be called Wonderful Counselor, Mighty God, Everlasting Father, Prince of Peace. Of the greatness of his government and peace there will be no end. He will reign on David's throne and over his kingdom, establishing and upholding it with justice and righteousness from that time on and forever. The zeal of the Lord Almighty will accomplish this. (Isa 9:6–7)

Very significantly the Holy Spirit, through Matthew, included four women, Tamar, Rahab, Ruth and Bathsheba (Uriah's wife), chosen by God in the fulfilment of the prophecy that Jesus was to be of the lineage of David. All four women had failed in keeping the covenant relationship that God had made with His people, starting with Abraham. But they had key positions in the royal line of descent of the Messiah. Neither their Gentile connections (Hittite/Moabite) nor the wrong actions of their past sinful lives had resulted in God's excluding them from eventually fulfilling such key roles in the birth of the Messiah. Yet each of these four could have, humanly speaking, been unable to fulfil this role due to unforeseen occurrences in any one of their lives, since that would break the chain of lineage.

We know little more about Tamar, but she must have repented and sought forgiveness in order to have become a mother in Israel and be given this position in the royal genealogy as ordained by God. She had resorted to this immoral act of seducing her father-in-law because he failed to keep his promise to her. Equally well, Bathsheba and Rahab had finished with their past sinful lives and sought a place with the people of God. They were chosen by God who knows all things, especially human sinful hearts, to be included in His plan and have their names in the royal lineage list, indicating that God was satisfied as to their relationship with Him. The Almighty continuously monitors all the steps in His plan to be able to take any evasive action that may be needed and there is always an open door, back to God, for those who confess and repent of their sins.

The Birth of the Messiah

God's plans for the coming of the Messiah were already made from eternity and so through the prophet, Isaiah, He declared:

> Therefore the Lord himself will give you a sign: The virgin will conceive and give birth to a son, and will call him Immanuel. (Isa 7:14)

Matthew, in his Gospel account, was led by the Holy Spirit to record the fulfilment of this prophecy (Matt 1:22), consistent with what he wrote in the rest of the chapter. Over the years, a great deal of debate has centred around whether the Greek word *parthenos*, translated to English as virgin, means a virgin not having had sexual relations or merely a young woman. So, for example, D.A. Carson has listed six reasons for questioning the historicity of the virgin birth and four theological considerations regarding this same event (Carson 1978, 71–74). It is not clear as to how many of these he supports because he lists a large number of commentators who speculate and offer alternative views rather than accept the direct statements of God's Word.

Both Matthew and Luke have used the Greek word *parthenos* in their Gospel records. This is also supported by the transliterated Hebrew word, *almah*, from the Hebrew MSS on which the Greek translation (the Septuagint) is based. In Matthew's account we are told that Mary was found to be with child before she and Joseph came together (Matt 1:18). Furthermore, both Matthew's and Luke's accounts emphasise that the birth was through the Holy Spirit (Matt 1:18; Luke 1:35). The pregnancy of Mary was explained to her, "before they came together," as being through the Holy Spirit (Matt 1:18).

Why is there any question, then, that Mary was still a virgin when Jesus was born? It is because some scholars prefer to exalt their own reasoning above the wisdom of God, going against the teaching that, "all Scripture is God-breathed" (2 Tim 3:16). God is the author of Scripture; the writers are instruments He uses. The ultimate authority for the truth of what is written lies with God, the author, not with the instrument He has used to record the message. Is it not significant that amongst the MSS found in the Dead Sea Scrolls, two were copies of Isaiah's MSS which have now been dated so as to go back to the days when our Lord Jesus taught His disciples from this text? (See my book in the Bibliography for further details of these matters.)

In His work Jesus was fulfilling the Isaianic prophecy:

> Here is my servant, whom I uphold, my chosen one in whom I delight; I will put my Spirit on him, and he will bring justice to the nations. He will not shout or cry out, or raise his voice in the streets. A bruised reed he will not break, and a smoldering wick he will not snuff out. In faithfulness he will bring forth justice. (Isa 42:1–3)

The Messiah had been chosen by God. He is God's Servant, anointed with God's Spirit to carry out a unique work. His work will be done with calmness and in peace, without force or violence and in care and consideration of the needy, to help and support them. This work, being the Lord's work, will result in victory and lasting changes. At the moment, the nations are obsessed by greed for power and wealth and often use violence to achieve their ends. Therefore such a work will be achievable only by the Lord's Servant who alone can bring about such a change in the fallen nature of man.

The Magi

Whether they were astrologers or astronomers is not clear from tradition but the account in Matthew (2:1–12) tends more towards their being astronomers. As we examine the account there are many factors in favour of describing them as a God-fearing group. Clearly they had no Jewish ancestry and perhaps little knowledge of the Old Testament Scriptures and so must have come to believe in the true and living God through the working out of the Scripture, "since what may be known about God is plain to them, because God has made it plain to them. For since the creation of the world God's invisible qualities—his eternal power and divine nature—have been clearly seen, being understood from what has been made, so that people are without excuse" (Rom 1:19–20). They recognised this babe was special as He had been revealed to them as King of the Jews. Not only had they travelled many miles at great cost and risk but they had also come prepared to worship Him, with choice gifts appropriate for a king (gold and frankincense) but also with an indication that there might be suffering and death ahead (myrrh). God continued to guide them until they arrived at the house where the Baby Jesus and Mary were staying, here they bowed down to Him and worshipped Him. God's hand continued guiding them because they were warned in a dream not to return to Herod but rather to go directly home.

In spite of this factual account of the Magi, a number of commentators have suggested that Matthew invented such stories to bolster the greatness of Jesus. Others suggest that Matthew created the stories to act as fulfilments of a group of testimonia texts taken from the Old Testament and being prophecies relating to the coming of the Messiah (see Morris 1992, 34). As a believer in the truth and reliability of the Scriptures, these suggestions are totally unacceptable to me. Matthew refers ten times to the fact that God's words were fulfilled just as He had said. There are ten references to the fulfilment of God's words spoken by the prophets in the Old Testament. These are referred to by Matthew in his Gospel 2:15, 17, 23; 4:14; 8:17; 12:17; 13:35; 21:4; 26:56 and 27:9. In all these references the authority of the statement is either the Lord or His prophets. There have been false prophets in the history of Israel, but the crucial test still stands, "If what a prophet proclaims in the name of the Lord does not take place or come true, that is a message the Lord has not spoken. That prophet has spoken presumptuously, so do not be alarmed" (Deut 18:22). The prophet is God's mouthpiece and so God puts in the heart and mind of the true prophet what he is to proclaim, and we, His people, need to judge and assess what is said by the prophet.

Closely connected with the visit of the Magi is the incident of the slaughter of the infants and of Bethlehem being the town where Jesus was born (Luke 2:4, 6–7). There was a popular misconception among some of the Jews that Jesus was born in Galilee (John 7:41–42). But though Jesus was born in Bethlehem, soon after the visit of the Magi the angel of the Lord instructed Joseph to take Mary and the babe and go to Egypt in order to escape Herod's murderous intentions. When Herod had died, the angel of the Lord appeared again to Joseph in a dream and instructed him to return to Israel. But when he returned to Judea, he discovered that Herod's son was reigning, and the angel of the Lord instructed him to settle in Galilee.

There now follow four interconnected prophecies in which Matthew has focussed attention on the prediction-fulfilment pattern he sees in the prophecies:

> 1. "In Bethlehem in Judea," they replied, "for this is what the prophet has written: 'But you, Bethlehem, in the land of Judah, are by no means least among the rulers of Judah; for out of you will come a ruler who will shepherd my people Israel. (Matt 2:5–6)
>
> 2. And so was fulfilled what the Lord had said through the prophet: "Out of Egypt I called my son." (Matt 2:15)

> 3. Then what was said through the prophet Jeremiah was fulfilled: "A voice is heard in Ramah, weeping and great mourning, Rachel weeping for her children and refusing to be comforted, because they are no more." (Matt 2:17–18)
>
> 4. And he went and lived in a town called Nazareth. So was fulfilled what was said through the prophets, that he would be called a Nazarene. (Matt 2:23)

In all four prophecies the emphasis is placed on the wording, "through the prophet." This is also true of the first prophecy even though some translations, such as the NIV, have omitted the preposition for "through" (Greek: *dia*). It is also to be noted that we cannot find the words, "He would be called a Nazarene," in the Old Testament, but this prophecy must have been known to Matthew for him to include it here. The Apostle Paul also made three references without citing the source in 1 Cor 7:10, 9:14 and Acts 20:35, so he must have known the origin and reliability of his sources.

It does not take too much imagination to see that any naturally occurring change could result in any one prophecy not being fulfilled. Equally well, it can be visualised that if any of the details of the occurrence of the visit of the Magi, the reaction of Mary and Joseph to having to move again and again, Herod's outrage, the stay in Egypt, all the connected journeys, with the permutations and combinations of these events leave open an almost endless number of possibilities leading to any one prophecy not being fulfilled, but for the powerful hand of the Almighty.

Looking through many commentaries (there are a considerable number referred to in Carson's bibliography on Matthew on pages 41 to 49) it is very common that fulfilment is sought by looking for one-to-one application or by the use of typology. I would draw attention instead to Jesus's own citations in Matt 21:12–17; Mark 11:15–19; Luke. 9:45–46 and John 2:12–16. Here He has conjoined two verses. The first verse is:

> These I will bring to my holy mountain and give them joy in my house of prayer. Their burnt offerings and sacrifices will be accepted on my altar; for my house will be called a house of prayer for all nations. (Isa 56:7)

In this verse, God promises that those living by His rules will be brought to His holy mountain and will be given joy "in my house of prayer." Their sacrifices will be accepted "for my house shall be called a house of prayer for all nations." The second verse is:

> Has this house, which bears my Name, become a den of robbers to you? But I have been watching! declares the Lord. (Jer 7:11)

In this verse, God points out to Israel that after committing all kinds of abominable Baal idolatry and worship, they dare to have the audacity to come to God's house, which bears His name, treating it as a "den of robbers." God's house is not a place, says Jesus, to stash or enjoy the fruits of illicit gain. Clearly Jesus is telling us that we cannot live wicked lives including the committing of idolatry and then come and stand unrepentant and expect to be accepted by God. Jesus shows us how the Old Testament messages need to be used in the New Testament as His Holy Spirit makes the Scriptures apply to us. He shows us through His servant, Matthew, how to be instructed by the Old Testament Scriptures as to God's purposes for our lives, bearing in mind that idolatry is not only connected with objects of wood, stone or precious metals, rather it is things or persons getting a priority in our lives beyond that which we give to God.

Let us look now and see how Matthew has been led to deal with the conjoined fulfilment prophecy concerning the Messiah in chapter 27:9–10. In the two Old Testament passages:

> I told them, "If you think it best, give me my pay; but if not, keep it." So they paid me thirty pieces of silver. And the Lord said to me, "Throw it to the potter"—the handsome price at which they valued me! So I took the thirty pieces of silver and threw them to the potter at the house of the Lord. (Zech 11:12–13)

and

> And Jeremiah said, "The word of the Lord came to me, saying, 'Behold, Hanamel the son of Shallum your uncle will come to you, saying, "Buy my field which *is* in Anathoth, for the right of redemption *is* yours to buy *it*."'" Then Hanamel my uncle's son came to me in the court of the prison according to the word of the Lord, and said to me, 'Please buy my field that *is* in Anathoth, which *is* in the country of Benjamin; for the right of inheritance *is* yours, and the redemption yours; buy *it* for yourself.' Then I knew that this was the word of the Lord. So I bought the field from Hanamel, the son of my uncle who *was* in Anathoth, and weighed *out to* him the money— seventeen shekels of silver. (Jer 32:6–9)

In these verses we do not see a one-to-one comparison between Jesus's betrayal, Zechariah's being undervalued for his services and Jeremiah being instructed to buy a field which was significantly undervalued because of the existing siege of Jerusalem by Nebuchadnezzar, king of Babylon. Matthew was shown that in these two undervaluations there was a recognition that the Messiah also was undervalued at a mere 30 pieces of silver by "the children of Israel" (Matt 27:9).

In this, Matthew saw the fulfilment of the prophecy that the Messiah who would come to deliver His people would be valued by them at a mere 30 pieces of silver. This was also the amount of compensation to be paid to the owner of a slave by the owner of a bull that accidentally gored the slave to death (Exod 21:32). The prophecy was ascribed to Jeremiah, probably because he was the major of the two prophets. Some commentators have ridiculously suggested that the attribution to Jeremiah is a copyist's mistake in the text of the Old Testament, and many have assumed that Matthew made a minor error (see Carson 1978, 563). They clearly have a low value of the text of the Scriptures and of Matthew's ability to handle records, even though he had spent many years keeping records and collecting taxes.

The Ministry of Jesus

Every step in the life of Jesus was carefully planned to achieve the purpose of doing His Father's will and to secure our eternal salvation. As seen in Isaiah, Jesus was anointed for this special ministry:

> The Spirit of the Sovereign Lord is on me, because the Lord has anointed me to proclaim good news to the poor. He has sent me to bind up the brokenhearted, to proclaim freedom for the captives and release from darkness for the prisoners, to proclaim the year of the Lord's favour and the day of vengeance of our God, to comfort all who mourn, and provide for those who grieve in Zion—to bestow on them a crown of beauty instead of ashes, the oil of joy instead of mourning, and a garment of praise instead of a spirit of despair. They will be called oaks of righteousness, a planting of the Lord for the display of his splendor. (Isa 61:1-3)

Very significantly when doing the Sabbath reading in the synagogue at Nazareth, Jesus was given the scroll of Isaiah and He found this portion of Scripture and read it aloud to them (Luke 4:16–21). He changed the wording as He read and omitted the "day of vengeance of God" and replaced it with "the year of the Lord's favour." When He sat down, He said to them, "Today this scripture is fulfilled in your hearing" (Luke 4:21). By His healing, preaching, deliverance from Satanic bondage and even raising the dead, He was fulfilling this prophecy. There was nothing in Isaiah's prophecy that Jesus did not fulfil. One significant change that He made to Isaiah's prophecy was that He was now proclaiming "the year of the Lord's favour" and not at this stage declaring "the day of vengeance." As Peter proclaimed in one of his sermons, "how God anointed Jesus of Nazareth with the Holy Spirit and power, and how he went around doing good and healing all who were under the power of the devil, because God was with him" (Acts 10:38).

Isaiah was given significant insights into the life and death of the Messiah, the most memorable revelation being in chapter 53. Soon after the prophecies describing the birth of the Messiah in chapter 7, there followed three prophecies related to Jesus's ministry in which though He was a king, He assumed the position of a Servant to His disciples as He washed their feet. Isaiah therefore reveals Him as the Servant-King. Ever since the invasion by Assyria, the northern regions of Israel were occupied by people from other countries (Gentiles). God had revealed to Isaiah as much as 600 years in advance, that Christ's light would shine on these people as Jesus took the Gospel to them (Matt 4:14–16).

Even when life is nearly extinguished, God has promised:

> A shoot will come up from the stump of Jesse; from his roots a Branch will bear fruit. (Isa 11:1)

and Jeremiah also prophesied that:

> "The days are coming," declares the Lord, "when I will raise up for David a righteous Branch, a King who will reign wisely and do what is just and right in the land. In his days Judah will be saved and Israel will live in safety. This is the name by which he will be called: The Lord Our Righteous Savior. (Jer 23:5–6)

Through the slender line of the genealogy, Jesus the Branch and the Fruit fulfilled the prophecy but wherever there is sin and a rejection of God's offer, judgement will follow. The same Rock that can be a refuge for those who trust Him can be a snare and a trap for those who have no fear of Him:

> The Lord Almighty is the one you are to regard as holy, he is the one you are to fear, he is the one you are to dread. He will be a holy place; for both Israel and Judah he will be a stone that causes people to stumble and a rock that makes them fall. And for the people of Jerusalem he will be a trap and a snare. Many of them will stumble; they will fall and be broken, they will be snared and captured. (Isa 8:13–15)

Jesus Himself referred to His rejection by the Jews by referring to the prophecy:

> The stone the builders rejected has become the cornerstone; the Lord has done this, and it is marvelous in our eyes. (Ps 118:22–23)

A little later He explained that the situation could be more serious by saying that, "Anyone who falls on this stone will be broken to pieces; anyone on whom it falls will be crushed" (Matt 21:44). Jesus regularly experienced vehement opposition from the Jews, so much so that on a number of occasions they sought to kill Him and told Him that He was mad and under the influence of Beelzebub, the prince of devils. They fundamentally disagreed with Him on issues concerning the Sabbath, healing and His claim to Deity. Towards the end of His life they openly rejected Him and in the presence of Pilate they chose a condemned criminal in preference to Him, so great was their hostility and hatred. Here two prophecies were fulfilled, the first:

> He was despised and rejected by mankind, a man of suffering, and familiar with pain. Like one from whom people hide their faces he was despised, and we held him in low esteem. (Isa 53:3)

He came in humility, fulfilling the second prophecy which was in Zechariah:

> Rejoice greatly, Daughter Zion! Shout, Daughter Jerusalem! See, your king comes to you, righteous and victorious, lowly and riding on a donkey, on a colt, the foal of a donkey. (Zech 9:9)

Jesus never used His Divine power to frighten or terrify those who sought to harm Him because He knew that His life was completely in the hands of His Heavenly Father. There were times when "all spoke well of him" (Luke 4:22) and yet within the hour, they were ready to "throw him off the cliff" (Luke 4:29). On another occasion when in His home town they asked the question, "Where did this man get this wisdom and these miraculous powers?" (Matt 13:54). He was just a carpenter's son, they said, and they despised Him. Yet, He continued day by day, healing and teaching in love and compassion because He saw them as "sheep without a shepherd" – they were harassed and helpless. Once again, He afforded His people the opportunity to welcome Him as their King. The people seemed to welcome Him, but it was short lived and fickle because a few days later they were crying, "Crucify him." On experiencing such hatred from the Jews, Jesus said to His disciples, "If I had not done among them the works no one else did, they would not be guilty of sin. As it is, they have seen, and yet they have hated both me and my Father. But this is to fulfill what is written in their Law: 'They hated me without reason'" (John 15:24–25). Now Jesus applied the words from the Psalms of David:

> Do not let those gloat over me who are my enemies without cause; do not let those who hate me without reason maliciously wink the eye. (Ps 35:19)

And,

> Those who hate me without reason outnumber the hairs of my head. (Ps 69:4)

So much unreasonable hatred was driven by uncontrolled anger. There was no consideration given to all the good, the healing, the teaching and perfect love that Jesus showed even to those who violently opposed and hated Him. When Jewish royalty were transported, they used mules to emphasise their status, as did Absalom and Solomon, but for Jesus only a donkey was found, emphasising His humility and how He became the servant of all. Though Jesus is the King of Kings, He became the Servant-King, even laying down His life for the salvation of mankind. Isaiah portrayed Jesus as the Servant of the Lord:

> After he has suffered, he will see the light of life and be satisfied; by his knowledge my righteous servant will justify many, and he will bear their iniquities. (Isa 53:11)

On the memorable occasion when Jesus in His humility washed His disciples' feet just before the Passover feast, He showed His disciples the full extent of his love by laying aside His outer garments and washing even the feet of

Judas, the traitor. This was to be the hallmark of Christian service, given by Jesus to His own for all time.

Fulfilment of the Scriptures

Almost synonymous with the fulfilment of prophecy is the fulfilment of the Scriptures, thereby encompassing all the words spoken by God. God's words are true and they never fail. The first sin of humankind came about by doubting and disobeying God's words. In this age we primarily receive God's words to us through the Scriptures. Any word received by whatever means that is not in agreement with the Scriptures would constitute breaking the Scripture (see John 10:35). Not accepting all that God has said and making exceptions for what we call "good" reasons or because we claim it does not apply is also breaking the Scripture. James makes this point in his letter (Jas 2:10–11), stating that even stumbling at one point while keeping the rest of the law makes a person guilty of breaking the whole law. Any word spoken by God is as good as God Himself. In order to reinforce His Word, "When God made his promise to Abraham, since there was no one greater for him to swear by, he swore by himself, saying, "I will surely bless you and give you many descendants." And so after waiting patiently, Abraham received what was promised" (Heb 6:13–15). In fact, Jesus made it clear that the fulfilment of the Scripture was so that when that which has been prophesied comes about, "you may believe that I am who I am" (John 13:19).

Jesus alone fulfilled all the prophecies and Scriptures that were written about Him over a period of at least 2000 years and so He alone is entitled to say to His disciples, "I am who I am." Jesus tells us so clearly the reason for His prophetic prediction is that, "when it does happen you will believe" (John 14:29). After all, God did not need to make prophetic utterances through His prophets, He did it to build up our faith in how great a God He is and, if necessary, we can lay down our lives for Him. His promise to keep His Word assures us that He will fulfil all His promises. There are many weaknesses in humans that result in our failing to keep our promises, but of Him we read, "God is not human, that he should lie, not a human being, that he should change his mind. Does he speak and then not act? Does he promise and not fulfill?" (Num 23:19). This is the story of the history of Israel as they settled in the land promised to their forefathers, "Not one of all the Lord's good promises to Israel failed; every one was fulfilled" (Josh 21:45). We sometimes read that Jesus, knowing certain events had been prophesied of Him, fulfilled them by precipitating the action required in the prophecy. So we read, "Later, knowing that everything had now been finished, and so that Scripture would be fulfilled, Jesus said, "I am thirsty." A jar of wine vinegar was there, so they soaked a sponge in it, put the sponge on a stalk of the hyssop plant, and lifted it to Jesus' lips" (John 19:28–29). Then a little later, "When he had received the drink, Jesus said, 'It is finished.' With that, he bowed his head and gave up his spirit" (John 19:30). To the very end even in His death, He was fulfilling what the Scriptures had stated about Him and ensured that the truth determined His actions expressed in the words, "But how then would the Scriptures be fulfilled that say it must happen in this way?"

(Matt 26:54). Some events occurred in the normal course of things but in order to fulfil His eternal purposes, He stepped in to ensure that they did occur as was planned, since when Christ came into the world He said, "Then I said, 'Here I am—it is written about me in the scroll—I have come to do your will, my God.'" (Heb 10:7), this being taken from:

> Then I said, "Here I am, I have come—it is written about me in the scroll. I desire to do your will, my God; your law is within my heart. (Ps 40:7–8)

Once again, none but Jesus could so satisfy and fulfil the will of God from the heart.

The Crucifixion

It is here that we see the foreknowledge and wisdom of our God in operational control. There were many events and many individuals whose movements were closely coordinated for the crucifixion to proceed according to God's will and in accordance with the prophecies given over a period of about 2000 years. Each event had a number of independently occurring, controlling factors which could alter the timing of the event and therefore the timing of the prophecies. For example, the sharing out of His garments at the crucifixion and the number of soldiers had to match one another so that they would have to cast lots for the undergarment (Mark 15:24; John 19:23–24). Anything could have happened to change the number of soldiers on duty for Jesus's crucifixion or the number of garments He was left with after His scourging and that, humanly speaking, could have affected the working out of the prophecy.

Could Judas have had a change of heart and not gone through with the betrayal? Humanly speaking, yes, but it was foreordained by God and therefore was not going to change. The 30 pieces of silver agreed perfectly with the number that had been prophesied. When Judas decided to betray Jesus, he went to the chief priests and asked for money, and there we read, "So they counted out for him thirty pieces of silver" (Matt 26:15c). Did the chief priests have any idea to fulfil prophecy or was it not our all-knowing God, working out what He had planned all along?

It is so significant to observe that when Jesus was predicting His betrayal, He referred to the Scripture:

> Even my close friend, someone I trusted, one who shared my bread, has turned against me. (Ps 41:9)

The Scriptural reference to Judas lifting up his heel against Jesus seems to fulfil the prophecy that the serpent will strike the heel of Jesus (Gen 3:15). We are told that after Jesus had washed His disciples' feet He indicated that one of them would betray Him. This one was identified as Judas and upon this identification we read, "As soon as Judas took the bread, Satan entered into him." (John 13:27). The devil found an opening into Judas's life because of his greed for money and through this the devil struck at the heel of Jesus at such a critical time in His life as He was preparing to go to the cross.

Jesus was flanked on both sides at His crucifixion by criminals also being crucified. The mob had asked Pilate to crucify Jesus whereas Pilate wanted to release Jesus and crucify Barabbas instead. Pilate's wife wanted him to have nothing more to do with Jesus. God's providential hand overruled and Jesus finally fulfilled prophecy as He was crucified with two criminals, one on each side and Jesus in the midst. In the midst of this miscarriage of justice prophecy was fulfilled again because we read, "This took place to fulfill what Jesus had said about the kind of death he was going to die" (John 18:32). The death of Jesus had to be at the hands of the Romans, only then would a death by crucifixion fulfil the prophecies made about Him. It was not an accident that the Jews were in the situation that they did not have the legal right of execution. Equally well, the Romans did not use crucifixion as a death penalty except for the category of being a criminal (that is how they classified Jesus). Pilate through weakness had given in to their demands but God's purposes were fulfilled. The events that occurred at the cross were deeply moving and extensively supported by covering prophecies. A master plan of God underlay all men's actions, ensuring that only what God wanted would happen.

Leading up to the Cross

In these last few days of His life on earth, before He died on the cross, Jesus experienced a period of intense suffering. The disciples had failed to support Him at Gethsemane and would once again desert Him as He went to the cross to fulfil the will of the Father. But He still thought of the needs of His disciples as He cited the prophecy from Zechariah:

> "Awake, sword, against my shepherd, against the man who is close to me!" declares the Lord Almighty. "Strike the shepherd, and the sheep will be scattered, and I will turn my hand against the little ones. In the whole land," declares the Lord, "two-thirds will be struck down and perish; yet one-third will be left in it. This third I will put into the fire; I will refine them like silver and test them like gold. They will call on my name and I will answer them; I will say, 'They are my people,' and they will say, 'The Lord is our God.'" (Zech 13:7-9)

Then Jesus told them, "This very night you will all fall away on account of me, for it is written: 'I will strike the shepherd, and the sheep of the flock will be scattered.'" (Matt 26:31). Jesus Himself amended this prophecy from its original application in Zechariah where it applies to a remnant, some of whom will be "struck down and perish", whereas the remainder will be purified and restored. In Jesus's use of this prophecy ("for it is written") all the disciples fell away but were later restored. I see with great reassurance that not only did Jesus amend the wording of the text from the Masoretic Text as found in Zechariah but also this amended wording was preserved in our Greek New Testament for nearly 2000 years. See my book in the bibliography for background information in this area of study. This shows how accurately the text of our New Testament has been transmitted and that words were not amended or added as people saw fit or thought they knew better than God. Jesus was giving hope to His disciples by warning them of their impending desertion of Him. For Peter who had failed catastrophically, Jesus had two reassuring messages. The first was that as the great High

Priest, Jesus had prayed for Peter and the second was that in spite of his denial of Jesus, He still had a place and a job for Peter in His kingdom (Luke 22:31–32). This tender concern of Jesus was also displayed by Him at the cross before He died as He committed His mother, Mary, to the care of the disciple, John. Only the greatest of the great could at such a time as this have the largeness of heart to fulfil the prophecy,

> The Spirit of the Sovereign LORD is upon me, because the LORD has anointed me ... to bind up the brokenhearted ... to comfort all who mourn. (from Isa 61:1–2)

Now it was Judas's turn to treacherously betray his Master, who although He knew from the beginning of Judas's intentions, treated him just the same as the other disciples. Judas was the subject of a number of prophecies and so with these in mind Jesus explained to His disciples the significance of the events that were occurring. First, He reminded them that at a mere word from Him, His Father would send twelve legions of angels (that is 12 times 6000) to rescue Him. Second, "But how then would the Scriptures be fulfilled that say it must happen in this way?" (Matt 26:54). This was fulfilled just as was prophesied because all the disciples deserted Jesus and fled (Matt 26:56). The Father, the Son and the Holy Spirit all working together made God's prophetic words to be fulfilled. Judas was warned of the gravity of his offence by Jesus on the occasion of the last supper (Mark 14:21). We are also solemnly told that as soon as it was revealed to the disciples that Judas would betray Jesus, that Satan entered into him (John 13:27). After Judas died, the Holy Spirit revealed through Peter that Judas had forfeited his position as an apostle:

> May their place be deserted; let there be no one to dwell in their tents. (Ps 69:25)

and his place was to be taken by another,

> May his days be few; may another take his place of leadership. (Ps 109:8)

Is this not a miraculous testimony to the working of the Holy Spirit that within a few short years, the fisherman Peter was now finding prophecies in the less well-known portions of the Scripture that applied to this complex situation and that needed a special revelation from God to meet this need? Was this not a fulfilment of the promise given in John 14:26 as the Holy Spirit taught Peter the things that were written in the Scriptures?

Still leading up to the cross, we now look at the false witnesses and their accusations. The Sanhedrin (a body of religious leaders) were seeking false witnesses because they were intent on putting Jesus to death. At first no two witnesses could agree on the alleged accusations until two of them said, "This fellow said, 'I am able to destroy the temple of God and rebuild it in three days.'" (Matt 26:61). We also have the prophetic prayer of David:

> Do not turn me over to the desire of my foes, for false witnesses rise up against me, spouting malicious accusations. (Ps 27:12)

But Jesus did not respond to these accusations and even though challenged by the High Priest, the Scripture states,

"But Jesus remained silent" (Matt 26:63). Jesus also told Caiaphas, the High Priest, that he and all of them would in the words of Revelation 1:7, see Him coming with the clouds, "and 'every eye will see him, even those who pierced him'; and all peoples on earth 'will mourn because of him.' So shall it be! Amen." This was entirely in keeping with Isaiah's prophetic utterance:

> He was oppressed and afflicted, yet he did not open his mouth; he was led like a lamb to the slaughter, and as a sheep before its shearers is silent, so he did not open his mouth. (Isa 53:7)

It is when one is oppressed and afflicted that the need is felt to cry out for justice, but Jesus not only knew that He was acting in accordance with the prophetic word, but also that this was His Father's will. Not only did Jesus die for us to secure our acceptance with God, but He also suffered for us. Having taken flesh and blood, He was made complete in His humanity by experiencing suffering as we humans do (Heb 2:10, 14, 18), but the extent of this suffering cannot be fathomed by us since we cannot visualise all that was involved in His death. Jewish flogging was restricted to 40 lashes, but the Roman crucifixion was brutal and barbaric, ensuring only that the victim had just enough strength to proceed to the next stage. Isaiah portrayed Jesus as, "a man of suffering, and familiar with pain" (Isa 53:3).

But we need to consider the possibility that Jesus could have still given His life under a Jewish regime by being stoned to death or pushed headlong down a cliff as the Jews did sometimes try to do (Luke 4:29; John 10:31). But our

Almighty God had predetermined that Jesus would experience a barbaric death, the details fitting only a Roman crucifixion in order to fulfil the prophecies made. In addition to flogging, Jesus was subjected to mocking and jeering. "Those who passed by hurled insults at him, shaking their heads and saying, "You who are going to destroy the temple and build it in three days, save yourself! Come down from the cross, if you are the Son of God!" … He trusts in God. Let God rescue him now if he wants him, for he said, 'I am the Son of God.'" (Matt 27:39–40, 43). How mocking and cutting were their taunts, accurately prophesied by the psalmist, David:

> All who see me mock me; they hurl insults, shaking their heads. "He trusts in the Lord," they say, let the Lord rescue him. Let him deliver him, since he delights in him. (Ps 22:7–8)

To add to it all there He hung on the cross, naked and bleeding and being taunted by the creatures He had created and for whose salvation He was now giving His life.

On the Cross

It was all in the purposes of God that two criminals were crucified alongside Jesus, one on His right and the other on His left. It was at this point that Jesus uttered His prayer, "Father, forgive them, for they do not know what they are doing" (Luke 23:34). It was either this prayer or what he had seen before, that may have touched the heart of the criminal who realised the evil of reviling Jesus, as others had reviled Him. Turning to Jesus, his request was that Jesus would remember him when He came into His kingdom. He was one soul snatched from destruction in the last moments of his life. Isaiah had been told by God that Jesus would be, "numbered with the transgressors" and that He, "made intercession for the transgressors" (from Isa 53:12).

Jesus derived strength to endure from the knowledge that He could entrust "himself to him who judges justly" (1 Pet 2:23). The casting of lots for Jesus's garments would have been out of the question if He had been stoned or thrown off a steep hill by a Jewish regime death. John's Gospel is very explicit as to the procedure followed, there were four soldiers and they divided His outer garments into four shares but the inner garment was "woven in one piece from top to bottom" (John 19:23b). Rather than tear it into four pieces, they cast lots to decide who would have it. In this account it is revealed to us that they were perfectly fulfilling the prophecy which said:

> They divide my clothes among them and cast lots for my garment. (Ps 22:18)

All the details of this prophecy were perfectly fulfilled because there were four soldiers, four outer garments and one seamless inner garment.

The soldiers now reached the stage of affixing the body of Jesus to the wooden cross. Here I recommend that the reader refers to Frederick Zugibe's book (Zugibe, 2005) in which two differing methods of crucifixion are mentioned, but only one conforms to the gospel account. The critical point of difference in the two lies in the point of attachment of the hand to the wooden cross. Zugibe, a medical practitioner and pathologist, defends the procedure indicated in the prophecy:

> Dogs surround me, a pack of villains encircles me; they pierce my hands and my feet. (Ps 22:16)

Psalm 22 is a powerful Messianic psalm and the many prophecies therein can apply to no other than the Messiah. Iron nails of the type used in Roman crucifixions have been found at Roman occupation sites in the East. Frederick Zugibe has included pictures of some of the nails given to him because of his long-term interest and publications on the subject of Jesus's crucifixion. Both John and Luke make clear reference to the piercing of the palms and feet of Jesus. After His resurrection, Jesus appeared first to Thomas. "Then he said to Thomas, 'Put your finger here; see my hands'" (John 20:27). Later He appeared to the other disciples and said to them, "Look at my hands and my feet. It is I myself! Touch me and see; a ghost does not have flesh and bones, as you see I have" (Luke 24:39). It should be noted here that Jesus would not expect His disciples to put their arms into His side, rather, their fingers would feel the wounds in His hands and side, even though the transliterated Greek word *cheir*, can mean arm as well as hand in various lexicons and concordances. The context here allows only 'hands' to apply to this situation.

Jesus was now getting near to the climactic hour of His time on the cross. It was at this point that it seems that God Himself acted in a series of successive spectacular occurrences against this heinous crime. At about the sixth hour, the sun stopped shining and darkness covered the whole land until the ninth hour; this was too long for a naturally occurring eclipse. The curtain of the temple separating the Holy Place from the Most Holy Place was torn in two from top to bottom – not from bottom to top as a human would have done. There then followed a violent earthquake and the tombs of many holy people burst open and after Jesus's resurrection, they appeared to many in Jerusalem. Even the hardened Roman centurion and his fellow guards who were in attendance at the crucifixion exclaimed, "Truly this man was the Son of God". A trigger occurred at the sixth hour of the day when darkness covered the land and Jesus cried out with a loud voice, "Eli, Eli, lema sabachthani?" that is, "my God, my God, why have you forsaken me?" (Matt 27:46). These were the very words David had prophetically used in Psalm 22 where he said:

> My God, my God, why have you forsaken me? Why are you so far from saving me, so far from my cries of anguish? (Ps 22:1)

The effect of this cry was that one of those standing by mistakenly thought that He called for Elijah. This was also the cue for a bystander to offer Jesus some wine vinegar which He refused in order to remain in total control during these final hours. Is it not amazing that even such a detail was both prophesied and fulfilled? Speaking prophetically, David says:

> They put gall in my food and gave me vinegar for my thirst. (Ps 69:21)

Shortly after comes the significance of what was happening, "Later, knowing that everything had now been finished, and so that Scripture would be fulfilled, Jesus said, "I am thirsty" (John 19:28) and shortly after this He uttered those memorable words, "It is finished" and dismissed His spirit. Once again the prophetic word appears to remind us that prophecy was being fulfilled by Divine intervention.

The Jews, in accordance with Divine instructions (Deut 21:22-23), did not want the bodies left on the crosses overnight and the Romans allowed the Jews this concession. Not only were the Jews now fulfilling the Law of God with the Romans agreeing to this, but our God ensured that everything worked out in accordance with His plan. The practice of the Romans was to break the legs of those being crucified to hasten death. This was done for the other two crucified with Jesus, but as He appeared dead already, just to be certain one of the soldiers thrust a spear into the side of Jesus and saw that both blood and water flowed out. (See Zugibe, 2005 for a medical explanation).

Not only do we have the eye witness of John but also the explanation that:

> These things happened so that the scripture would be fulfilled: "Not one of his bones will be broken," (John 19:36)

And also this prophecy is taken from another of David's psalms under the inspiration of the Holy Spirit:

> He protects all his bones, not one of them will be broken. (Ps 34:20)

By dismissing His spirit when He did, it was not necessary for the soldiers to break His legs. Was it an accident that Joseph of Arimathea, a rich man, secured the body of Jesus from Pilate and had the body embalmed and laid in his own new tomb? Or, was this action fulfilling the prophecy from Isaiah?

> He was assigned a grave with the wicked, and with the rich in his death, though he had done no violence, nor was any deceit in his mouth. (Isa 53:9)

I see the hand of God giving this rich man, who was a secret disciple, the courage to step forward and fulfil what God had said would happen.

A question that is raised by some is to ask why Jesus felt so forsaken by His Father and the answer is clearly to indicate that it was because He was dying as the sin bearer for sins we had committed as He bore God's judgement. We continue at the cross as we see further prophecies fulfilled. The words of Scripture in this connection are so penetrating when it states, "God made him who had no sin to be sin for us, so that in him we might become the righteousness of God" (2 Cor 5:21).

His Resurrection, Exaltation and Glorification

In the final phase of the life of the Messiah we consider the bearing of prophecy on the resurrection, exaltation and glorification of the Messiah. The prophecies concerning the resurrection and exaltation were given through David in the Psalms, "you will not abandon me to the realm of the dead, nor will you let your faithful one see decay"

(Psalm 16:10) and "The Lord says to my lord: 'Sit at my right hand until I make your enemies a footstool for your feet" (Ps 110:1).

These were the verses that Peter used at Pentecost to show from the Scriptures that the Messiah who the Jews had put to death by crucifixion was now alive and at the right hand of the Father in the position of authority and power. These prophecies were also cited by Jesus Himself as He stood in front of the Sanhedrin and said, "I say to all of you: From now on you will see the Son of Man sitting at the right hand of the Mighty One and coming on the clouds of heaven" (Matt 26:64). These words of Jesus contain a hint of the enthronement of the Son of Man:

> In my vision at night I looked, and there before me was one like a son of man, coming with the clouds of heaven. He approached the Ancient of Days and was led into his presence. He was given authority, glory and sovereign power; all nations and peoples of every language worshiped him. His dominion is an everlasting dominion that will not pass away, and his kingdom is one that will never be destroyed. (Dan 7:13–14)

This vision is described fully in Revelation chapter 21, where He is again honoured and given authority, glory and sovereign power and all people worshipped Him – because His dominion and kingdom are everlasting. This prophecy is yet to be fulfilled in full measure as every knee will bow to Him and every tongue will confess His name. The main emphasis in prophecy is not to specify the time when it will be fulfilled, rather it is to indicate the one who is at the heart of the prophecy and what the Almighty will do. This statement is amply supported by the incident in which Jesus met two disillusioned disciples (Luke 24:17–35). They had been slow of heart to believe what the prophets had said, also they did not realise that Christ had to suffer before He entered His glory. So beginning with Moses and the prophets, He explained to them the meaning of the prophecies concerning Himself in the Scriptures. This is what opened their eyes and made their hearts burn. This reinforcement of the message of prophecy must have shown the disciples the importance that Jesus attached to the role of prophecy in building up the faith of disheartened disciples.

Jesus emphatically stated that only the Father made the decision for the time of His Second Coming. Perhaps, this is why the books of Daniel and Revelation, which have so much to tell us about the future, give time spans in enigmatic forms. God wants us to know that these life-changing events will certainly occur, but we need to be prepared for their occurrence at any time – just as certainly as death comes to humans or Jesus returns, whichever is sooner, but we do not know exactly when it will happen. Jesus nevertheless gave us signs that we may become aware as the day of His return draws nearer. His words are more certain of fulfilment than even the survival of heaven and earth. Amongst the signs He has given us is that from the prophecies of Daniel:

> After the sixty-two 'sevens,' the Anointed One will be put to death and will have nothing. The people of the ruler who will come will destroy the city and the sanctuary. The end will come like a flood: War will continue until the end,

> and desolations have been decreed. He will confirm a covenant with many for one 'seven.' In the middle of the 'seven' he will put an end to sacrifice and offering. And at the temple he will set up an abomination that causes desolation, until the end that is decreed is poured out on him. (Dan 9:26–27)

God had shown Daniel a great amount of what was going to happen to the Messiah (the Anointed One) but as before, the time spans are enigmatic. Jesus especially wanted us to understand the significance of these events with regard to the end times (Matt 24:15). A full account of the historical fulfilment of Daniel's prophecy can be seen in Bruce 1963, 222–225. After the siege of Jerusalem, the city was taken in 70 CE and this was followed by the capture of the fortress, the cessation of the daily sacrifice, the destruction of most of the walls of the city and the temple. The last straw in this desecration was the act of the Roman soldiers setting up their legionary standards in the temple court and offering sacrifices to them. This action was viewed by many as the abomination of desolation prophesied by Daniel.

It was also at this time that the prophecy given by Jesus to His disciples was fulfilled. This relates to the temple at Jerusalem:

> "Do you see all these things?" he asked. "Truly I tell you, not one stone here will be left on another; every one will be thrown down." (Matt 24:2b)

There was some discussion by Titus, the Roman commander, during this siege of Jerusalem as to whether the magnificent temple itself should be saved from destruction but events overtook such considerations and Jesus's words were fulfilled.

In this chapter (Matt 24) Jesus also answers the question of His disciples, "Tell us," they said, "when will this happen, and what will be the sign of your coming and of the end of the age?" (verse 3b). Jesus answered their question by saying that deceivers would come claiming "I am the Christ" and many will be deceived. Then alarm will be created by wars and rumours of wars as nations fight one another. There will also be famines and earthquakes, but this is just the start. Because of Jesus, many will be persecuted and killed, resulting in betrayal, hatred and falling away. Wickedness will increase and the love of most will grow cold, but the message of the gospel will spread worldwide. Jesus said that at this time the hearers need to understand the significance of the occurrence of the abomination of desolation spoken of by Daniel. The hardship and distress will be the greatest ever known. Deceivers will even have miraculous powers, but all the people will also see the Son of Man coming with power and great glory as He collects His own from the four corners of the universe. These signs, said Jesus, will precede His coming but no one knows the day or even the hour. He then referred to the account of Noah and the flood to make the crucial point that we all need to be ready, always! Underlying our need to be constantly ready is the basic principle of our personal accountability to our Master, who may return any moment and require an account of us. By being prepared for His return, we will be constrained to live orderly lives and as reminded, we ought to live holy and godly lives, as we look forward to the day of God (see 2 Pet 3:11–12). Jesus does not give any time line or order of sequence to these events but points out that they are signs of the end time.

We continue to see in wonder and admiration as Jesus is raised from humiliation and death to the highest heights of glory and being acknowledged as King of Kings and Lord of Lords. At some stage in the future known only to God, Jesus will come to the earth with the voice of the archangel and the trumpet call of God. The dead in Christ will rise first and after that, we who are still alive and are left will be caught up together with them in the clouds to meet the Lord in the air (1 Thess 4:16–17). After this comes the time for the judgement of the enemies of Christ as He comes with the armies of heaven to judge and make war (Rev 19 onwards).

The enemies are defeated and the beast and false prophet are thrown into the fiery lake of burning sulphur. Satan is locked in a bottomless pit for one thousand years (the Millennium). Those who were given authority to judge reigned with Christ for the one thousand years and this is the first resurrection. The second death has no power over them. When the one thousand years have been completed, Satan will be released and will gather the nations to fight against God and His people. The enemies of God will be destroyed by fire from heaven and the devil will be finally thrown into the lake of burning sulphur. The great white throne now comes down from heaven and all the dead are judged according to what they had done. If anyone's name was not written in the Book of Life, he was thrown into the lake of fire.

A new heaven and earth now appear in which God will dwell with His people. There will be no more sorrow, crying, pain or death for those who are His. The new Jerusalem and the bride of the Lamb are now revealed from heaven. The Lord God Almighty and the Lamb are its temple and its glory and those dwelling in it are the ones whose names are written in the Lamb's Book of Life. Our human minds can only dimly comprehend the glories of the Lamb and the new age He has prepared for us. We are exhorted at the very beginning of Revelation to heed what is written in it and to take it to heart. As an apocalyptic book it is not easy to understand its details and therefore it can easily be ignored. But we need to know that this is "the revelation of Jesus Christ" and He has promised a blessing to those who heed His message that He is coming soon. We do not know the actual time when He will come and trigger the cataclysmic changes that follow. But it certainly will happen because He has said, "You also must be ready, for the Son of Man is coming at an hour you do not expect" (Luke 12:40).

So after examining more than 50 prophecies in detail and finding each one precisely fulfilled in spite of so many factors that, humanly speaking, could have resulted in failure, we are confronted with the evidence that the fulfilment was as God had predicted through His prophets. In this book I have sought to show the powerful evidence presented by fulfilled prophecy in the life of Jesus the

Messiah, so convincingly fulfilled that the evident conclusion is that this is the Word of God speaking to us.

Bibliography

Carson, D. A. Matthew: Expositors' Bible Commentary. Editor Frank E. Gabbelein. 1978.

Morris, Leon. The Gospel According to Matthew. 1992.

Bejon, Cushroo. The Word of God in Our Hands. 2018.

New Bible Dictionary. Second Edition. 1982.

Bruce, F.F. The Time is Fulfilled. 1978.

Zugibe, F. T. The Crucifixion of Jesus. 2005.

Nicole, Roger. New Testament Use of the Old Testament, in Revelation and the Bible. Edited by Carl F.H. Henry. 1958.

Grogan, G.W. 'The New Testament Interpretation of the Old Testament' in Tyndale Bulletin (1967) 18:54-76.

Bruce, F.F. The New Testament Development of Old Testament Themes. 1968.

Gundry, R. H. The Use of the Old Testament in Saint Matthew's Gospel. 1967.

Gabbelein, Frank E. The Old Testament in the New Testament. The Expositors' Bible Commentary. 1979.

Earle E. Ellis. How the New Testament Uses the Old. New Testament Interpretation. Edited by I. Howard Marshall. 1985.

Bruce, F. F. Israel and the Nations. 1963.

www.ingramcontent.com/pod-product-compliance
Lightning Source LLC
Chambersburg PA
CBHW061514040426
42450CB00008B/1618